Business Analy

I0016404

Dr.Hiriyappa.B, Ph.D.

Contents

· · · · · · · · · · ·

1

Introduction to Analytics

. . . .

Information is considered the lifeblood of any business, irrespective of its size. For the growth and development of the businesses, analysis of data becomes essential. An organization that makes large investments must invest time in **data analytics** to make better business decisions. Today, analytics has become an indispensable component for businesses and organization to stay competitive and relevant. Business analytics and big data has become one of the main functional areas in most business organizations. Business analytics consists in the study, analysis, and interpretation of big data of organizations and businesses. It is an important component of management science. In today's age of the Internet, e-commerce and social media existence have increased the complexity of the data relating to business. Business analytics uses statistical operations research and management tools to drive business performance. Traditional systems lacked data analysis capabilities because of limited business transactions and data required for decision-making. On the other hand, today, business transactions have created problems due to limited ability of the human mind to analyze the various possibilities of solutions and the limited time available for decision-making. The biggest obstacle to adopting analytics is the lack of knowledge as to how to use it to improve business performance.

Analytics helps you understand how people use your websites, blogs, and apps, so you can take action to improve their experience. analytics that give you an instant status on your website's health, mishaps, and opportunities.

Business analytics is designed to provide in-depth knowledge of business analytic techniques and their applications in improving business processes and decision-making. This book helps in determining business problems; collecting and analyzing alternative choices of solutions; and interpreting data to inform business decisions, identify and recognize trends, detect outliers, summarize data sets, analyze relationships between variables, develop and test hypotheses, find outcomes of the business, improve performance of the business, and devise competitive strategies for an organization.

Analytics

The term 'analytics' is very popular in the Internet, business research, and information technology. It became very relevant in the e-business, e-governance, e-data management, data mining and sharing, and e-commerce scenarios. Business analytics uses statistical, operations research and management tools to drive business performance. Analytics has been defined as the extensive use of data, statistical and quantitative analysis, explanatory and predictive models, and fact-based management to drive decisions and actions. Analytics is a field that combines data, information technology, statistical analysis, quantitative methods, and computer- based models into one. These are combined to provide decision makers all the possible scenarios to make a well thought out and researched decision. The computer-based model ensures that decision makers can see the performance of their decisions under various scenarios.

It is a process of transforming data into actions through analysis and insights in the context of organizational decision-making and problem solving. Analytics includes a range of activities, including business intelligence, which comprises standard and ad hoc reports; queries and alerts; and quantitative methods, including statistical analysis, forecasting/extrapolation, predictive modeling such as data mining, optimization, and simulation.

Analytics is more than just analytical methodologies or techniques used in logical analysis. It is to gain an understanding of how managers use business analytics to formulate and solve business problems and to support managerial decision-making. It is to become familiar with the processes needed to develop, report, and analyze business data.

2
Business Analytics

· ·

Business analytics is a set of techniques and processes that can be used to analyze data to improve business performance through fact- based decision-making. Business analytics create capabilities for companies to compete in the market effectively. There is striking correlation between an organization's analytics sophistication and its competitive performance. Many companies offer similar kinds of products and services to customers based on similar design and technology and find it difficult to differentiate their product/ service from their competitors. However, nowadays companies use analytics as competitive strategy of the business.

Business analytics helps companies to find the most profitable customer and allows them to justify their marketing effort, especially when the competition is very high. By using the business analytical software, the corporate world has the ability to make better decisions, and it improves with analytical skills.

Decision-making process is largely dependent on business analytics in organizations and businesses. When business analytics is carried out the right way, it can help companies put the right foot forward.

Business analytics is based on the data and statistical methods. It focuses on using a set of metrics to investigate the past, present, and future of an organization or a business.

Business analytics is the process of making sense of gathered data, measuring business performance, and producing valuable conclusions that can help companies make informed decisions on the future of the business, using various statistical methods and techniques.

Business analytics is associated with business intelligence. Business intelligence is related to the collection of data and find toward understanding the company current circumstances and situation. Business intelligence is querying, reporting, online analytical processing (OLAP), and "alerts." Meanwhile the concern of business analytics is putting all that data into use and explains the reasons for the situations: it is the bridge that connects the technical side of the business with the managerial, decision-making side of it.

Business analytics refers to the skills, technologies, practices for continuous iterative exploration and investigation of past, present and predict and prescription of business performance to gain insight and drive business planning to achieve goals and objectives. Business analytics focuses on developing new insights and understanding of business performance based on information, events, transactions, circumstance data and statistical tools, methods. In contrast, business intelligence traditionally focuses on using a consistent set of metrics to both measure past performance and guide business planning, which is also based on information, events, transactions, circumstance data and statistical tools, methods.

Business analytics makes extensive use of analytical modeling and numerical analysis, including explanatory, description, prescription and predictive modeling, and fact-based management to drive business planning and decision-making. It is therefore closely related to management science. Analytics may be used as input for human decisions or may drive fully automated decisions.

In other words, querying, reporting, OLAP, these are alert tools that can answer questions such as what happened, how many, how often, where the problem is, and what actions are needed. Business analytics can answer questions like why is this happening, what if these trends continue, what will happen next (predict), and what is the best outcome that can happen (optimize) to make the best decision.

Business analytics is a combination of data analytics, business intelligence and computer programming. It is the science of analyzing data to find out patterns that will be helpful in developing strategies. Its usage can be found in almost every industry.

Evolution of business analytics

Business analytics has been existence since very long time and has evolved with availability of newer and better technologies. It has its roots in statistics and operations research, which was extensively used during World War II. Operations research and statistics was an analytical way to look at data to conduct military operations. Over a period of time, this technique started getting utilized for business. Here statistics and operation's research evolved into management science. Again, basis for management science remained same as statistics and operation research in data, decision-making models, etc.

As the economies started developing and companies became increasingly competitive, management science evolved into business intelligence, business analytics, computer programs help decision support systems and into PC software.

Scope of business analytics

Business analytics has a wide range of application and usages. It can be used for descriptive analysis in which data are utilized to understand past and present situation. This kind of descriptive analysis is used to assess current market position of the company and effectiveness of previous business decision.

It is used for predictive analysis, which is typical used to assess future business performance.

Business analytics is also used for prescriptive analysis, which is utilized to formulate optimization techniques for stronger business performance.

It is to gain an understanding of how managers use business analytics to formulate and solve business problems and to support managerial decision-making.

It is to become familiar with the processes needed to develop, report, and analyze business data.

It is to learn how to use and apply Excel and Excel add-ins to solve business problems.

It explain how data are used for recruiting and performance evaluation

Its model supply and demand for various business scenarios It

helps to solve business problems with data-driven decision-making

It helps you to understand the tools used to predict customer behavior

You gain skills such as predictive analytics, customer analytics, regression analysis and marketing performance measurement and management.

Importance of business analytics

Business analytics is a methodology or tool to make a sound commercial decision. Hence it impacts functioning of the whole organization. Therefore, business analytics can help improve profitability of the business, increase market share and revenue, and provide better return to a shareholder.

Facilitates better understanding of available primary and secondary data, which again affect operational efficiency of several departments.

Provides a competitive advantage to companies. In this digital age flow of information is almost equal to all the players. It is how this information is utilized makes the company competitive. Business analytics combines available data with various well thought models to improve business decisions.

Converts available data into valuable information. This information can be presented in any required format, comfortable to the decision maker.

For example, business analytics is used to determine pricing of various products in a departmental store based past and present set of information.

Data use foranalytics

Business analytics uses data from three sources for construction of the business model. It uses business data such as annual reports, financial ratios, marketing research, etc. It uses the database which contains various computer files and information coming from data analysis.

3

Challenges of
Business Analytics

. . . .

Collection of data becomes challenging task for an organization's existing IT systems to ingest, store, process and analyze it. Data collection is increasing volume, velocity, variety, and veracity of the data; it is a huge challenge to manage the data and get the relevant business insights and intelligence from it. You can find the relevance of business analytics solutions which utilizes specialized software tools and applications for descriptive, predictive, prescription analytics, data mining, forecasting, and optimization.

Business analytics focuses on developing new insights and understanding of business performance based on data and statistical, operation research methods and computer program used to find the data, predict, and make decision-making how to handle data in business development, growth, and survival of business.

Benefits and advantages of implementing business analytics

After implementation of business analytical in businesses, you get various benefits from business analytics and its impact on business as follows:

Business analytics can help improve profitability of the business, increase market share and revenue, and provide better return to a shareholder.

Descriptive analytics examines different types of data and how it can be visualized in the business.

Predictive analytics explores the potential uses of data once they are collected and interpreted and accurately transferring information to business.

Prescriptive analytics takes you to the point of formulizing concrete recommendations of what you should do for accomplish goals and objectives of business. It brings consequent improvement in efficiency and helps to portray future challenges.

Business analytics can help companies make strategic decisions on the future of the business.

It is a data science which consists in a perfect blend of data science and analytics through the use of various statistical methods and techniques.

Business can use either free analytical or commercial analytical software so that it reduces the cost and time.

Business analytical reports can share information with a larger audience and ease in sharing information with stakeholders and moreover, any technology is subject to its own set of problems and challenges.

Business analytical helps entrepreneurs and almost anyone using data science to generate insights by unearthing patterns and by decoding these data. These insights are helping to improve efficiency and to offer innovative solutions to business problems.

It involves faster reporting, analysis, or planning, which is more accurate reporting, analysis or planning and take the better business decisions by using the improved data quality.

Business analytical brings the improved employee satisfaction, improved operational efficiency, improved customer satisfaction, increased competitive advantage and finally reduced the cost of operation of business. it results that increased revenues, and saved headcount.

Challenges in implementing business analytics in an organization

Business analytics success purely depends on all parties of an organization fully support adoption and execution.

Proper management of structured and unstructured data in an organization.

Collaboration of business, IT personnel and among the cross-functional analytics team that includes major players in technology, business, operations, legal, and HR can help full-scale adoption of analytics in every department must be in-sync for an analytics strategy to succeed.

Lack of commitment of many analytics software packages provider's initiative in implementation of analytical and executives are losing the trust during the period of implementation of analytical software so that the team must set process and goal must establish a productive analytics environment and set realistic timelines for results.

BA implementations often fail due to lack or low quality of available data, Acute shortage of professionals who understand big data analysis.

A maturity assessment should always be performed on the company's information architecture and data sources based on analytical requirements. Transactional, aggregated, and operational information should be scored for quality, and the existing integration infrastructure's ability to support new sources and data feed should be evaluated.The time required to acquire, clean, and analyze new data must be built into the adjustment period.

Uncertainty of data management landscape, data storage and quality, business analytics is too expensive, lack of adoption by team members, Measuring the wrong indicators, data overload, lack of technical skills in employees, data security and maintenance, Integrity of data, delivering relevant information in the given time, Inability to address complex issues and lack of a proper strategy to implement BA.

Getting meaningful insights through the use of big data analytics and failure to make strategic decisions happens due to dearth of professionals who're well equipped with the knowledge of business analytics.

A business analytical professional can take up corporate roles in various sectors: marketing, insurance, management, finance, health care, lifestyle, etc. In fact, there is still hesitation to use trends and statistics for making business decisions, and most of them still are comfortable trusting their gut feeling for making strategic decisions.

Business analytics can be possible only on large volume of data. It is sometime difficult obtain large volume of data and not question its integrity.

4

How Business Analytics Helps Companies

. . . .

The goal of business analytics is to determine which datasets are useful and how they can be leveraged to solve problems and it enables businesses to understand the current market scenario and change the process or trigger a need for new product development that matches the market needs, thereby increasing efficiency, productivity, and revenue of companies.

How business analytics helps a company

Analyzing data allows understanding of both the business and the industry more specifically; business analytics provides clarity of business, helps know where a company stands in the industry, and gives clarity to develop effective strategies to making decision. Analyze the data as per competitiveness of similar companies and prescribe the timeliness to easy and fast decision-making that yields positive results.

It helps in understanding the current state of the business or process and provides a solid foundation to predict future outcomes.

Description, predictive, and prescription analytical are pillars of analytics and how they help provide insights and lead to better decision-making in business of an organization.

It helps to companies to take faster and better business decisions.

It helps to companies to be improved business performance with real-time monitoring of events.

It helps to companies to be increased product and service development.

It helps to companies to become to take competitive advantage in the industry.

It helps to companies to take better identification of risks and effective mitigation.

It helps to companies to provide improved customer engagement.

It helps to companies to find the skills, technologies, practices for continuous iterative exploration and deep investigation of past business performance of the respective company and also the competitors to gain insight and drive business planning in an effective way.

It helps companies to totally focus on developing new insights into or awareness and full understanding of the business performance of own organization and also the competitors in the market based on data and statistical methods. Indifference and intelligence in the past completely focuses on using a continuous set of metrics to both calculating past performances and also act as complete hand guide for business planning, which is also based on data, statistical, probability and mathematical methods. It also uses
– data science, data analytics, etc.

Business analytics helps to companies to makes large use of statistical analysis, includes appropriate explanatory and predictive modeling methods, and fact-based management and fixed data/ information driven based management to drive decision-making in a better way.

It is closely related to management science, data science, and data analytics. Analytics used as input for driven human decisions or may drive fully automated decisions.

It helps to companies to make querying, reporting, online analytical processing, and alerts. Customer analytics, people analytics and operations analytics.

It helps to company to keep them up-to-date in a changing environment by adopting latest industry trends and best practices.

It provides the needed knowledge for companies to survive in today's constantly changing business environment and providing a detailed look into various opportunities and challenges that companies face on a day-to-day basis.

It helps to companies to elevates pinpoint operational inefficiencies and respond to them accordingly.

It helps to companies to empowers businesses to be forecasting ability, which makes the business more agile and prepared for possible risks. As a result, the business is able to make important decisions with more confidence, knowing that it can handle the risks and adjust the consequences.

It helps to companies to builds stronger customer relationships with customer s and to create a better marketing strategy to nurture long and fruitful relationships with its customers.

It helps companies to allow the business to understand the environment in which it operates, to find out how it can become more competitive, to streamline the decision-making in the company, and to ultimately maximize its revenues.

5

Business Analytics Process

· ·

Business analytics is the real-time analysis. It is an emerging business tool that is changing the traditional methods of analytics. Business analytics tools are to enable by business enterprises and take proactive decision-making.

Business analytics tool is the flourishing because of applied in any industry where data are captured and accessible. These data can be used for a variety of reasons, ranging from improving customer service as well improving the organization's capability and performance to predict the future to offering valuable insights on online and digital information.

Business analytics process

Business analytics process is the steps or methods and tools involved that can be applied to any industry where data are collected, analyzed, interpreted and these event streams to support decision-making in organizations. Business analytics processes occur at all organizational levels and it may or may not be visible to the customers. Process of business analytics involved seven steps as outlined.

Step 1: Defining the business needs and requirement

The first stage in the business analytics process involves understanding what the business needs and how would like to improve on or solve problem. you should able to understand the purpose of your analysis and try to know what the business is and what the business is trying to achieve. So that you need the data. Data are collected into raw form and processed according to the requirement of a company and then these data are utilized for the decision-making purpose. This process helps the businesses to grow and expand their operations in the market. But the main question arises – what are the business needs? And finds the what are the requirement for the business. At this stage, key questions such as, "what data are available, "How can we use them," you can check "do we have sufficient data" for analytics.

Step 2:Explore the structured and unstructured data

This stage involves cleaning the data, making computations for missing data, removing outliers, and transforming combinations of variables to form new variables. we need to gather initial data such as structured and unstructured data, describe and explore data and lastly verify data quality to ensure it contains the data we require. Data collected from the various sources are described in terms of its application and the need for the project in this phase. This is also known as data exploration. This is necessary to verify the quality of data collected.

Once the data have been cleaned, the analyst will try to make better sense of the data. The analyst will plot the data using scatter plots (to identify possible correlation or non-linearity). He will visually check all possible slices of data and summarize the data using appropriate visualization and descriptive statistics such as mean, standard deviation, range, mode, median that will help provide a basic understanding of the data. At this stage, the analyst is already looking for general patterns and actionable insights that can be derived to achieve the business goal.

Step 3: Analyze the data

In research, once data are collected, the next step is to get insights from it. At this stage, it involved for obtaining raw data and converting it into information useful for decision-making by users. Data are processed, organized, and cleaned would be ready for the analysis. Various data analysis techniques are available to understand, interpret, and derive conclusions based on the requirements of the business and industry. Data are collected and analyzed to answer questions, test hypotheses prove or disprove theories. using statistical analysis methods such as correlation analysis and hypothesis testing, the analyst will find all factors that are related to the target variable. The analyst will also perform simple regression analysis to see whether simple predictions can be made. In addition, different groups are compared using different assumptions and these are tested using hypothesis testing. Often, it is at this stage that the data are cut, sliced, and diced and different comparisons are made while trying to derive actionable insights from the data. There are many different data analysis methods, depending on the type of research. Here are a few methods you can use to analyze quantitative and qualitative data.

Step 4:Predict what is likely to happen

In general, prediction is the process of determining the magnitude of statistical variates at some future point of time. Business analytics is about being proactive in decision-making. This technique used to make predictions about unknown future events. Predictive analytics uses many techniques from data mining, statistics, modeling, machine learning, and artificial intelligence to analyze current data to make predictions about at this stage, the analyst will model the data using predictive techniques that include decision trees, neural networks, and logistic regression. These techniques will uncover insights and patterns that highlight relationships and "hidden evidences" of the most influential variables. The analyst will then compare the predictive values with the actual values and compute the predictive errors. Usually, several predictive models are running and the best performing model selected based on model accuracy and outcomes. Forecasting refers to a process of looking forward, and predetermining future trends and the impact on the organization.

Step 5:Optimize to find the best solution

An optimization problem is the finding the best solution for problem from all feasible solutions for the problems. Optimization problems can be divided into two categories depending on whether the variables are continuous or discrete. In this stage, the analyst will apply the predictive model coefficients and outcomes to run "what-if" scenarios, using targets set by managers to determine the best solution, with the given constraints and limitations. The analyst will select the optimal solution and model based on the lowest error, management targets and his intuitive recognition of the model coefficients that are most aligned to the organization's strategic goal.

Step 6: Make a strategic decision and measure the outcome

The analyst will then make a strategic decision and act based on the long-term goals and a vision. Strategic decisions are intended to gain a competitive advantage that derived insights from the model and try to change the overall scope and direction of the organizational goals. At an appropriate period after this action has been taken, the outcome of the action is measured.

Step 7: Update the system with the results of the strategic decision

Finally, the results of the decision and action and the new insights derived from the model are recorded and updated into the database. Information such as, "was the decision and action effective?""How did the treatment group compare with the control group? "And "what was the return on investment? "are uploaded into the database. The result is an evolving database that is continuously updated as soon as new insights and knowledge are derived.

6

Types of
Business Analytics

. . . .

Business analytics is the process of collecting large chunks of structured/unstructured data, segregating and analyzing it. and discovering the patterns and other useful business insights from it. It helps in determining which data are relevant and can be analyzed to drive better business decisions in the future. Many commercial as well as open-source tools are available for business analytics in organizations. Nowadays, the amount of data collected is rising in every second and a high volume of data is being generated, it is only natural to have tools that will help us handle this information. Raw data are often a pile of unstructured information. Data analysts use their expertise to derive statistically significant information from the data. This is where different types of data analytics come into play. Data-driven insights play an integral role in helping businesses form new initiatives.

For different stages of business analytics huge amount of data is processed at various steps. Depending on the stage of the workflow and the requirement of data analysis, there are four main kinds of analytics – descriptive, diagnostic, predictive, and prescriptive. These four types together answer everything a company needs to know from what is going on in the company to what solutions to be adopted for optimizing the functions.

The big data revolution has given birth to different kinds, types, and stages of data analysis. Boardrooms across companies are buzzing around with data analytics - offering enterprise wide solutions for business success to understand what each type of analytics delivers to improve on, an organization's operational capabilities. Business analytics helps to business to understanding and selecting the right descriptive, predictive, and prescriptive analytics is by gaining the right information, which delivers knowledge, that gives businesses the power to gain a competitive edge. The main goal of business analytics is to help organizations make smarter decisions for better business outcomes.

Descriptive analytics

This is the branch of business analytics analyses and finds answer to the question,"What has happened in the past. "This can be termed as the simplest form of analytics. The purpose of this analytics type is just to summarize the findings and understand what is going on.

Descriptive analytics is the interpretation of historical data to better understand changes that have occurred in a business. Descriptive analytics describes the use of a range of historic data to draw comparisons. It gains insight from historical data with reporting and scorecards, clustering, and it easily understandable and interpretable by humans in terms of describing or summarizing the existing data using existing business intelligence tools such as arithmetic operations, mean, median, max, percentage, etc. on existing data. It is useful to better understand what is going on or what has happened.

This type of analytics is helpful in deriving any pattern if any from past events or drawing interpretations from them so that better strategies for the future can be framed.

This is the most frequently used type of analytics across organizations. It is crucial in revealing the key metrics and measures within any business.

Business analytics mainly involves descriptions based on aggregations of past performance. It is an important step to make raw data understandable to stake holders of business. It uses two primary techniques, namely data aggregation and data mining to report past events. It presents past data in an easily digestible format for the benefit of a wide business audience. This method is purely used for understanding the underlying behavior and not to make any estimations. By mining historical data, companies can analyze the consumer behaviors and engagements with their businesses that could be helpful in targeted marketing, service improvement, etc. The tools used in this phase are MS Excel, MATLAB, SPSS, STATA, etc.

A common example of descriptive analytics are company reports that simply provide a historic review of an organization's operations, sales, financials, customers, and stakeholders. Summarizing past events such as regional sales, customer attrition, or success of marketing campaigns.

Tabulation of social metrics such as Facebook likes, Tweets, or followers.

Reporting of general trends like hot travel destinations or news trends.

Predictive analytics

This branch of business analytics, this model uses forecasting techniques, statistical techniques, machine-learning techniques, and data science techniques to find out what is going to happen in future. Predictive analysis helps to business in predicting the future course of events and taking necessary measures for the same.

Predictive analytics helps businesses to forecast trends based on the current events. Whether it is predicting the probability of an event happening in future or estimating the accurate time it will happen can all be determined with business applications of predictive analysis such as risk assessment, sales forecasting, using customer segmentation to determine which leads have the best chance of converting. Predictive analytics in customer success teams the help of predictive analytical models.

Predictive analytics is used to predict future outcomes. However, it is important to note that it cannot predict if an event will occur in the future; it merely forecasts what are the probabilities of the occurrence of the event. A predictive model builds on the preliminary descriptive analytics stage to derive the possibility of the outcomes.

The essence of predictive analytics is to devise models such that the existing data are understood to extrapolate the future occurrence or simply, predict the future data. One of the common applications of predictive analytics is found in sentiment analysis where all the opinions posted on social media are collected and analyzed the existing text data to predict the person's sentiment on a particular subject as being positive, negative or neutral future prediction.

Hence, predictive analytics includes building and validation of models that provide accurate predictions. Predictive analytics relies on machine-learning algorithms like random forests, support vector machine, and so on and statistics for learning and testing the data. Usually, companies need trained data scientists and machine- learning experts for building these models. The most popular tools for predictive analytics include Python, R, Rapid Miner, etc.

The prediction of future data relies on the existing data, as they cannot be obtained otherwise. If the model is properly tuned, it can be used to support complex forecasts in sales and marketing. It goes a step ahead of the standard business intelligence in giving accurate predictions.

Diagnostic analytics

This branch of business analytics, this model uses a few techniques that uses diagnostic analytics such as attribute importance, principle components analysis, sensitivity analysis, and conjoint analysis. Training algorithms for classification and regression. It focuses on past performance to determine what happened and why. The result of the analysis is often an analytic dashboard.

Diagnostic analytical tools aid an analyst to dig deeper into an issue at hand so that they can arrive at the source of a problem.

In a structured business environment, tools for both descriptive and diagnostic analytics go hand-in-hand.

Diagnostic analytics is used to determine why something happened in the past. It is characterized by techniques such as drill- down, data discovery, data mining and correlations. Diagnostic analytics takes a deeper look at data to understand the root causes of the events. It is helpful in determining what factors and events contributed to the outcome. It mostly uses probabilities, likelihoods, and the distribution of outcomes for the analysis.

In a time, series data of sales, diagnostic analytics would help you understand why the sales have decrease or increase for a specific year or so. However, this type of analytics has a limited ability to give actionable insights. It just provides an understanding of causal relationships and sequences while looking backward.

Business applications of diagnostic analysis such as a freight company investigating the cause of slow shipments in a certain region. An SaaS company drilling down to determine which marketing activities increased trials.

Prescriptive analytics

This branch of business analytics, it recommends decisions making use of optimization, simulation algorithms, assumptions, etc. to find answer to the question," What should we do?" Prescriptive analysis is used to give advices on possible outcomes. This is a relatively new field of analytics that allows users to recommend several different possible solutions to the problem and to guide them about the best possible course of action.

It is a type of predictive analytics that is used to recommend one or more course of action on analyzing the data.

This type of analytics explains the step-by-step process in a situation. For instance, a prescriptive analysis is what comes into play when your Uber driver gets the easier route from Gmaps. The best route was chosen by considering the distance of every available route from your pick-up route to the destination and the traffic constraints on each road.

It can suggest all favorable outcomes according to a specified course of action and also suggest various course of actions to get to a particular outcome. Hence, it uses a strong feedback system that constantly learns and updates the relationship between the action and the outcome.

The computations include optimization of some functions that are related to the desired outcome. For example, while calling for a cab online, the application uses GPS to connect you to the correct driver from among a number of drivers found nearby. Hence, it optimizes the distance for faster arrival time. Recommendation engines also use prescriptive analytics.

The other approach includes simulation where all the key performance areas are combined to design the correct solutions. It makes sure whether the key performance metrics are included in the solution. The optimization model will further work on the impact of the previously made forecasts. Because of its power to suggest favorable solutions, prescriptive analytics is the final frontier of advanced analytics or data science, in today's term.

Decision analytics

This is branch of business analytics that supports human decisions with visual analytics that the user models to reflect reasoning. Decisions are driven by these analytics or we can say that this one is for drive decisions.

7

Business Analytics Tools for Business

. . . .

Business analytics tools for business helps in determining which data are relevant and can be analyzed to drive better business decisions in the future. Business analytics tools allow you to fully utilize your data by providing end users with visual representations of it, ultimately for full-fledged analysis.

Business analytics tools consist of a set of solutions, methods, skills, and best practices used to gain insights for understanding current business realities and business planning. The primary use of business analytics is to drive decision-making. Business analytics is heavily statistically focused and uses analysis techniques such as descriptive, predictive, and prescriptive analytics. Many commercial as well as open-source tools are available for business analytics in organizations.

They are two source of tools such as open-source tools and commercial source tools. Open-source tools get free and commercial source get paid. Most small and medium companies could not afford the high paid tool, and neither did it make sense for them to invest in it as their analysis needs were different. The companies that have and could use it, often ended up paying more for the tool than the analyst who worked on the tool and this was not an optimal scenario. Every analytics tool provider is designing tools with greater usability and self-service analytics. They want to alleviate the need to have data scientists on staff to get advanced analysis and model building done. Taking steps to make these changes helps users find quick solutions and streamline decision-making overall.

If we needed analytics to work for business the way we wanted need for industry-wide adoption of cheaper tools, and better if they were free.

In line with the growing importance of open-source tools in the field of analytics, I have decided to switch the order of listing the top tools. I will start with the most popular open-source tools this time and then move on to the commercial or paid tools.

There are many emerging technologies that enable deeper insights into data and the ways in which data are structured for analysis.

Analytical tools are frequently used by many industries for reporting and analysis. There are many analytical tools that are not listed in this that enterprises use such as forecasting models and simulations, but data mining is included since it is used by a wide range of businesses for data discovery. Many analytic tools are in high growth markets and are expected to be used in tandem with other analytical tools in the future.

Open-source analytics tools

Here are the five most popular open-source analytics tools:

R

R is now the most popular analytics tool in the industry. R is commonly known as 'R programming language' is an open-source programming language and R is a language and environment for statistical computing and graphics. It is basically used for statistical computations and high-end graphics. Therefore, it is a popular language among mathematicians, statisticians, data miners, and also scientists to do data analysis. R has the built-in universal statistical methods such as mean, median, distributions, covariance, regression, nonlinear mixed effects, GLM, GAM and the list just goes R provides a wide variety of statistical techniques such as linear and nonlinear modeling, classical statistical tests, time-series analysis, classification, clustering, etc. and graphical techniques, and is highly extensible. It is GNU software i.e. R is a GNU project, and is freely available under the GNU (General Public License), and R comes with pre-compiled binary versions for several operating systems ranging from Unix and similar systems (FreeBSD, Linux), Windows and MacOS. it is an operating system that is free software.

R programming as a flexible graphical environment to offer a wide variety of graphical functions for data presentations such as bar plots, pie charts, histograms, time series, dot charts, image plots, 3D surfaces, scatter plots, maps, etc. R programming is designed for data analysis, object oriented, it is interpreted as computer language and it provides advanced analytics.

R is an integrated suite of software facilities for data manipulation, calculation, and graphical display. It provides an effective data handling and storage facility, A suite of operators for calculations on arrays, in particular matrices, A large, coherent, integrated collection of intermediate tools for data analysis, Graphical facilities for data analysis and display either on-screen or on hardcopy, and a well-developed, simple and effective programming language which includes conditionals, loops, user-defined recursive functions and input and output facilities.

Python

Python is powerful, fast, plays well with others, runs everywhere, if friendly and easy to learn, is open, an interpreted, high-level, general-purpose programming language. Created by Guido van Rossum, Python has a favorite for programmers because of an easy to learn language that is also quite fast, write clear, logical code for small and large-scale projects.[. However, it developed into a powerful analytics tool with the development of analytical and statistical libraries. Today it offers a comprehensive coverage of statistical and mathematical functions.

Python offers applications are Web and Internet development database access, desktop graphical users' interface, scientific and numeric, education, network programming, software, and game development.

Web and internet development

Python offers many choices for web development:

Frameworks such as Django and Pyramid.

Micro-frameworks such as Flask and Bottle.

Advanced content management systems such as Plone and django CMS.

Scientific and numeric computing

Python is widely used in scientific and numeric computing:

SciPy is a collection of packages for mathematics, science, and engineering.

Pandas is a data analysis and modeling library.

IPython is a powerful interactive shell that features easy editing and recording of a work session, and supports visualizations and parallel computing.

The software carpentry course teaches basic skills for scientific computing, running bootcamps and providing open-access teaching materials.

Education

Python is a superb language for teaching programming, both at the introductory level and in more advanced courses.

Books such as How to Think Like a Computer Scientist, Python Programming: An Introduction to Computer Science, and Practical Programming.

The education special interest group is a good place to discuss teaching issues.

Business applications

Python is also used to build ERP and e-commerce systems:

Odoo is an all-in-one management software that offers a range of business applications that form a complete suite of enterprise management applications.

Tryton is a three-tier high-level general-purpose application platform.

Apache Spark

Apache Spark is a lightning-fast unified analytics engine for big data and machine learning. It was originally developed at UC Berkeley in 2009. Spark is another open-source processing engine that is built with a focus on analytics, especially on unstructured data or huge volumes of data. Spark has become tremendously popular in the last couple of years. This is because of various reasons – easy integration with the Hadoop ecosystem being one of them. Spark has its own machine-learning library which makes it ideal for analytics as well. Spark works on static data. Storm is ideal for real-time analytics or stream processing.

Apache Spark is an open-source distributed general-purpose cluster-computing framework. with (mostly) in-memory data processing engine that can do ETL, analytics, machine learning, and graph processing on large volumes of data. Spark provides an interface for programming entire clusters with implicit data parallelism and fault tolerance. it also works with the system to distribute data across the cluster and process the data in parallel.

Apache Spark has features such as speed to run application in Hadoop cluster, it supports multiple languages such as APIs, in Java, Scala, or Python, it uses advanced analytics supports such as streaming data, machine learning, and graph algorithms.

Apache Storm

Apache Storm is a free and open-source distributed real-time computation system. Apache Storm makes it easy to reliably process unbounded streams of data, doing for real-time processing what Hadoop did for batch processing. Apache Storm is simple, can be used with any programming language, and is a lot of fun to use!

Apache Storm has many use cases: real-time analytics, online machine learning, continuous computation, distributed RPC, ETL, and more. Apache Storm is fast: a benchmark clocked it at over a million tuples processed per second per node. It is scalable, is fault-tolerant, guarantees your data will be processed, and is easy to set up and operate.

Apache Storm integrates with the queueing and database technologies. An Apache Storm topology consumes streams of data and processes those streams in arbitrarily complex ways, repartitioning the streams between each stage of the computation however needed.

PIG and HIVE

PIG and HIVE are the two key components of the Hadoop ecosystem that reduce the complexity of writing Map-Reduce queries. Both these languages are like SQL.

PIG is a high-level programming language useful for analyzing large data sets. HIVE is a data warehouse infrastructure tool to process structured data in Hadoop.

PIG enables people to focus more on analyzing bulk data sets and to spend less time writing Map-Reduce programs. It resides on top of Hadoop to summarize big data, and makes querying and analyzing easy. It renders to a simple language called PIG Latin as a high-level data flow system that. Especially, which is used for data manipulation and queries. Moreover, to store the data we do not need to create the schema in PIG. Also, we can directly load the files and start using it. However, in PIG we can also sue semi- structured data which is the benefit of PIG.

Apache Hive is an open-source data warehouse system that has been built on top of Hadoop. It is used majorly for analyzing and querying large datasets that have been stored in Hadoop files. Hadoop Hive is used for processing structured and semi-structured data.

Features of Apache Hive Are Easy data summarization and analysis and query support, External tables are supported and making it feasible to process data without having to store it into HDFS, supports the partitioning of data at the data level for better performance, a rule-based optimizer present in Hive responsible for optimizing logical plans and The structured data can be processed in Hadoop using Hive. In Hive, adhoc queries can also be run for data analysis. It can use for easy extraction, transformation, and loading of data, it offers several tools. we can use and define custom mapper and reducer. It is useful for data analytics and reporting related work, it is most preferred.

Commercial analytics tools
Now, let's look at the five most popular paid analytics tools:

SAS
The SAS system. SAS stands for the Statistical Analysis System. It is a software system for data analysis and report writing. SAS is a leader in business analytics. SAS is a group of computer programs that work together to store data values and retrieve them, modify data, compute simple and complex statistical analyses, and create reports.

SAS is a statistical software suite developed by SAS Institute for advanced analytics, multivariate analysis, business intelligence, criminal investigation, data management, and predictive analytics. The drag-and-drop interface makes it easy for you to create better statistical models quickly. It has decent functional graphical capabilities.

Through our innovative, trusted technology and passionate connection to the progress of humanity, SAS empowers our customers to move the world forward by transforming data into intelligence.

SAS analytics U is the free offering for download for teaching, learning and research. SAS skills in programming, analytics, data science, administration, data management and enterprise business intelligence.

Tableau

Tableau is a powerful and fastest growing data visualization tool used in the business intelligence industry. It helps in simplifying raw data into the very easily understandable format. Data analysis is very fast with Tableau and the visualizations created are in the form of dashboards and worksheets. The data that is created using Tableau can be understood by professional at any level in an organization. It even allows a non-technical user to create a customized dashboard. The software comes in a desktop, server, and online hosted model. Tableau Public is free software that allows anyone to connect to a spreadsheet or file and create interactive data visualizations for the web. Tableau Reader is free and allows you to open and interact with data visualizations built-in Tableau Desktop.

The best features of Tableau are data blending, real-time analysis, and collaboration of data.

Tableau leverages visual analytics that enables users to interact with data. This practice helps users to visually interact with data to make crucial decisions and get faster insights. This is a very effective tool in creating interactive data visualizations rapidly. It is simple to use and user-friendly in nature. Tableau is the most powerful, secure, and flexible end-to-end analytics platform for your data. Designed for the individual, but scaled for the enterprise, Tableau is the only business intelligence platform that turns your data into insights that drive action.

Excel

Excel is of course the most widely used analytics tool in the world. Microsoft Excel is a spreadsheet program. That means it is used to create grids of text, numbers and formulas specifying calculations. That is extremely valuable for many businesses, which use it to record expenditures and income, plan budgets, chart data and succinctly present fiscal results. It is the most used spreadsheet program in many business activities, classwork, and even personal data organization.

QlikView

QlikView is one of the fastest evolving business intelligence (BI) and data visualization tool. QlikView is a BI data discovery product for creating guided analytics applications and dashboards tailor-made for business challenges. The software enables user to uncover data insights and relationships across various sources with QlikView's Associative data Indexing Engine. Qlik provides an end-to-end platform which includes data integration, user- driven BI and conversational analytics.

Splunk

Splunk produces software for searching, monitoring, and analyzing machine-generated big data, via a Web-style interface. Splunk (the product) captures, indexes, and correlates real-time data in a searchable repository from which it can generate graphs, reports, alerts, dashboards, and visualizations. Splunk is a horizontal technology used for application management, security, and compliance, as well as business and web analytics

Other business analytical tools

Common tools used in business analytics include Micro Strategy, SPSS, BIRT, Matomo, MetaBase, and OmniSci.

8

Business Analytics Applications

. . . .

Analytics companies develop the ability to support their decisions through analytic reasoning using variety of statistical and mathematical techniques. There is a significant proportion of high-performance companies have high analytical skills among their personnel. Advanced analytics tools have helped get deeper insights and discovery which will challenge assumptions made in business. Also, business analysts and users get more information and significant potential in creating business value and competitive advantage.

Business analytics applications an important benefit is that the use of data helps companies save so much money, develop better marketing strategies, improve the efficiency in procurement, support the growth of business and differentiate themselves from other competitors in the industry.

Business analytics applications

Business analytics applications in various fields. In fact, you will find its application in day-to-day activities too such as companies study the pattern of their consumers: their lifestyle, spending patterns, likes and dislikes through mundane activities such as clicks and shares on social networking sites like Facebook, Twitter, and Instagram. These data help them develop their advertising strategy and target the apt audience. Business analytics is used by companies to data-driven decision- making. Simply it is a study of data through statistical and operations analysis. The industries using business analytics on a day-to-day basis will help you understand various business analytical application which are uses in business.

Financial analytics

Business analytics is crucial to the businesses and finance sector. Financial analytics can help you understand your business' past and present performance and predict future performance to make better business decisions. Financial analytics software helps in speeding up the creation of reports and data presentation through graphs, which is much easier to read and comprehend. Financial analytics involves using massive amounts of financial and other relevant data to identify patterns to make predictions.

Financial analytics offers insight into organizations' financial status and improves the profitability, cash flow and value of the business. Financial analytics also helps companies improve income statements and business processes.

Financial analytics can help companies determine the risks they face, how to enhance and extend the business processes that make them run more effectively, and whether organizations' investments are focused on the right areas.

Financial analytical crucial because of businesses require timely information, every company needs prudent financial planning and forecasting, advancements in technology, all point to the need for financial analytics. Financial analytics can help shape up the business' future goals, improve the decision-making strategies for your business, focus on measuring and managing your business' tangible assets such as cash and equipment.

It provides an in-depth insight into the organization's financial status and improves the cash flow, profitability, and business value.

Human resource analytics

Human resource analytics is a data-driven approach to managing people at work. It also known people analytics, or HR analytics or Workforce analytics or talent analytics, by using various types of HR software and technology,

HR analytics is the science of gathering, organizing, and analyzing the data related to HR functions like recruitment, talent management, employee engagement, performance, and retention to ensure better decision-making in all these areas

HR analytics common data sources include internal data like demographic employee data, payroll data, social network data, performance data, and engagement data. External data sources can include labor market data, population data, LinkedIn data, and much more. Any data that is relevant for the specific project can be used.

Human resource analytics helps you how to improve performance, identify best performing talent, predict in demand skills and positions within the organizations, identify the attribution and causes, the transfer the role HR as a strategic partner.

HR analytical tools helps you to conduct relevant background checks on potential candidates, find out detailed information about employee attrition rate, high-performance candidates, and so on, to find information about educational background of high performing candidates, employee attrition rate, number of years of service of employees, age, gender, etc. This information can play a pivotal role in the selection procedure of a candidate.

Marketing analytics

Marketing analytics comprises the processes and technologies that enable marketers to evaluate the success of their marketing initiatives. This is accomplished by measuring performance (e.g., blogging versus social media versus channel communications). Marketing analytics is software which is used for the practice of measuring, managing, and analyzing marketing performance to maximize its effectiveness and optimize return on investment. it helps marketers gain a better understanding of their customers. Using business analytics in marketing helps companies target customer needs by focusing their messaging or timing of a certain product or service on what is best for the consumer it tells you how your marketing programs are really performing.

Marketing analytics gathers data about consumer behavior and market trends. identify target customers as well as potential markets, buying patterns of consumer behavior, analyzing trends, help in identifying the target audience, employing advertising techniques that can appeal to the consumers, forecast supply requirements from across all marketing channels and consolidates it into a common marketing view. Marketing analytics reveal vital statistics. It enables you to improve your overall marketing program performance by identifying channel deficiencies, adjusting strategies and tactics as needed, optimizing processes and gaining customer insight.

Marketing analytics helps you finds the marketing initiatives performing today, marketing activities compare with our competitors, marketing resources properly allocated

Health care analytics

Healthcare analytics is the collection and analysis of data in the healthcare industry by using the analytical software and technology. Healthcare analytics is the branch of analysis that focuses on offering insights into hospital management, patient records, costs, diagnoses, medical costs, clinical data, patient behavior, pharmaceuticals, it can be used on both macro and micro levels to effectively streamline operations, improve patient care, and lower overall costs and more in order to gain insights and support decision-making. Research and development are crucial aspects of healthcare, providing new innovative solutions and treatments that can be properly tracked, measured, and analyzed.

Supply-chain analytics

Supply-chain analytics is the application of mathematics, statistics, predictive modeling, and machine-learning techniques to find meaningful patterns and knowledge in order, shipment, and transactional and sensor data. Supply-Chain analytics is helping to improve operational efficiency and effectiveness by enabling data-driven decisions at strategic, operational, and tactical levels. The supply-chain is a great place to use analytic tools to look for a competitive advantage of businesses. Supply-chain analytics can help an organization make smarter, quicker, and more efficient decisions

An important goal of supply-chain analytics software is to improve forecasting and efficiency and be more responsive to customer needs.

Web analytics

Web analytics is the measurement, collection, analysis and reporting of web data for purposes of understanding and optimizing web usage. Web analytics provides information about the number of visitors to a website and the number of page views. Web analytics is the process of analyzing the behavior of visitors to a Web site. The use of Web analytics is said to enable a business to attract more visitors, retain or attract new customers for goods or services, or to increase the dollar volume each customer spends.

Its focus is on identifying measures based on your organizational and user goals and using the website data to determine the success or failure of those goals and to drive strategy and improve the user's experience.

CRM analytics

Customer relationship management (CRM) is used to describe an automated methodology of processing data about a customer to make better business decisions. CRM analytics are statistics or metrics that offer insights into areas like sales performance or customer service that show how a business is performing. These insights help companies make decisions to better serve customers, improve relationships, and increase sales.

CRM analytics comprises all programming that analyzes data about customers and presents it to help facilitate and streamline better business decisions.

9

Career in Business Analytics

. . . .

Business analytics generate employment opportunities and brings careers in data analyst, management consultant, big data specialist, operations research analyst and market research analyst.

Need for business analytics

To become business analytical analyst, you need the skills such as collaboration, ability to align with stakeholders, basic knowledge of stats tools such as Excel, and the ability to drive impact, working with operation research and computer programs relating with analytical testing skills.

Business analytical work done by business analysts. Business analysts are the people who have the needed knowledge, skills, and sources of information to decide on the direction the business needs to take to succeed in the future.

Career on business analytical purely depends on specialties include choosing the opportunities with the highest potential of success, calculating the strategy that would prove most fruitful for the business, or preparing the company for the upcoming change.

Business analyst specialization provides an introduction to business analytics for all business professionals, including those with no prior analytics experience. You will learn how data analysts describe, predict, and inform business decisions in the specific areas of marketing, human resources, finance, and operations, and you will develop basic data literacy and an analytic mindset that will help you make strategic decisions based on data. you will apply your skills to interpret a real-world data set and make appropriate business strategy recommendations.

Business analytical wide range of applications. Applies in various types of industries dealing with high levels of risk, for instance insurance, banking, networking, and information sharing companies, would apply analytics in their operations. As the data revolution changed the way of doing business, companies from all industries faced various kinds of risks which could only be avoided by the use of up-to-date, relevant information.

The person who has involved in the collecting for a piece of information to be useful, it needs to be processed, understandable, and actionable. This is why every piece of data that a business collects or stores needs to be analyzed by a person who knows how to use statistics to draw actionable and useful conclusions to get more opportunities.

Finally, analytics allows for fast and precise decision-making. Since time is everything in business, it is understandable why business analytics is considered the hottest occupation in the 21st century.

Nowadays, companies are realizing the importance of business analytics relative to their competitiveness and success has become the go-to job of this century.

That is to say: although every modern company needs someone to take care of its data, there are not enough professionals offering expert services to these companies to satisfy the demand.

Other professional easy to swift to business analytics that can be applied to any industry when it comes to business analytics.

Business analytics application can be applied to any industry such as sports, education, manufacturing, insurance, banking, automotive etc.

A career in business analytics is make professional development of analytical personal who continuously face various challenges as they operate in different environments and meet clients with specific needs and business analysts to stay in contact with people from different clients, with various skills and expertise, which enriches their knowledge.

Hence, business analysts continuously learn new things and find different techniques that produce more effective and innovative solutions to complex problems.

Careers in business analytics

A career in business analytics usually requires at least a bachelor's degree in business analytics, data science, information management, applied analytics, BI, statistics, marketing, or a related field. A master's degree can widen job choices and certifications can provide more authority and help increase value. Business analytical experts often report directly to upper management within their organization. They may be in a department of their own but coordinate closely with sales, marketing, and operations. Careers available in business analytics include management data analyst/scientist, BI analyst, program, and marketing managers, big data analytics specialist, operations research analyst, and market research analyst

www.ingramcontent.com/pod-product-compliance
Lightning Source LLC
Chambersburg PA
CBHW031249050326
40690CB00007B/1016